THE FEAR OF FAILURE.

How to become an action taker, stop worrying, and overcome procrastination and perfectionism.

By

Louie L Sanchez.

Table of content

Introduction

Chapter 1 **UNDERSTANDING YOUR FEAR. Common causes of fear for an individual.**

Chapter 2 How **TO CHANGE YOUR PERSPECTIVE.**

Chapter 3 **Get out of your head a way to overcome fear**

Chapter 4 **Master ingredients to great achievement**

Chapter 5 **Great ideas for dealing with fear and your inner critic**

BREAKING THE FEAR OF FAILURE

How to become an action taker, stop worrying, and overcome procrastination and perfectionism.

LOUIE.L SANCHEZ.

Table of content

Introduction

Have you ever been so hysterical about failing at a commodity that you decided not to try at all? Or has fear of failure meant that, subconsciously, you undermine your sweat to avoid the possibility of a larger failure?

multitudinous of us have presumably endured this at one time or another. But when we allow fear to stop our forward progress in life, we're likely to miss some great openings along the way,

In this composition, we'll examine the fear of failure, what it means, what causes it, and how to overcome it to enjoy true success in work, and in life Fear is a natural, important, and primitive mortal emotion that is touched off by perceived trouble. It's an introductory survival medium that signals our bodies to respond to pitfalls with a fight or flight response. Also, it's an essential part of keeping us safe

Fear is a natural response that is triggered by a perceived threat or danger. It is a survival mechanism that prepares our body to either fight or flee from the threat. When we experience fear, our amygdala, a small organ in the brain, activates our nervous system and releases stress hormones like cortisol and adrenaline. This leads to physical changes such as increased heart rate, elevated blood pressure, and rapid breathing.

Chapter 1
Understanding your fear

Understanding fear is crucial because it can have a significant impact on our lives. Some individuals thrive on fear, seeking out activities that provide a thrill or adrenaline rush. Others, however, avoid fear and try to stay within their comfort zones. The reason behind these different responses to fear can vary from person to person.

Fear can be both beneficial and detrimental. It is an important emotion that helps keep us safe by alerting us to potential dangers. However, excessive or irrational fear can interfere with our happiness, sense of security, and ability to function effectively. It can manifest as anxiety or phobias, limiting our potential and preventing us from living life to the fullest.

Learning to understand and manage fear is essential for personal growth and development. By recognizing the triggers

101010

and underlying causes of our fears, we can work towards overcoming them. This may involve seeking professional help, practising relaxation techniques, or gradually exposing ourselves to our fears in a controlled and supportive environment.

Several factors can cause fear in individuals. Here are some common causes:

1. Traumatic experiences: Personal experiences of trauma or witnessing traumatic events can lead to the development of fear. These experiences can create a lasting impact on an individual's psyche, causing them to associate similar situations or stimuli with fear.

2. Conditioning and learned fear: Fear can be learned through conditioning. For example, if someone has a negative experience or receives punishment in a specific situation, they may develop fear associated with that situation. This learned fear can also be passed on through observation or hearing about others' negative experiences.

3. Biological factors: Fear can also have a biological basis. The amygdala, a part of the brain responsible for processing emotions, plays a crucial role in fear responses. Genetic factors and imbalances in brain chemicals like serotonin and dopamine can also contribute to the development of fear disorders.

4. Cultural and societal influences: Cultural and societal factors can shape an individual's fears. For example, certain phobias may be more prevalent in specific cultures due to cultural beliefs, superstitions, or exposure to certain environmental factors.

5. Media and information exposure: Exposure to frightening or distressing content through media, such as movies, news, or social media, can contribute to the development or intensification of fears. Graphic or sensationalised portrayals of certain situations or events can create a sense of fear or anxiety in individuals.

6. **Personal beliefs and perceptions**:
Individual beliefs, thoughts, and
perceptions can also contribute to the
development of fear. Negative self-talk,
irrational thinking patterns, or distorted
perceptions of reality can amplify fears and
make them seem more threatening than
they are. It's important to note that fear can
vary in intensity and duration among
individuals. While fear can be a normal and
adaptive response to certain situations,
excessive or irrational fears can interfere
with daily life and may require professional
help to manage.

This fear may not have a specific cause or
trigger, but it affects your overall well-being
and can manifest in various ways. It may
stem from past traumas, unresolved
emotions, or deep-seated anxieties.
Subconscious fear can be challenging to
identify and address, as it operates on a

171717

subconscious level. However, it is important to acknowledge and work through this fear to live a more fulfilling and balanced life.

When we experience fear, our brain activates the amygdala, which is responsible for processing emotions, including fear. The amygdala then sends signals to various parts of the body, triggering a cascade of physiological changes.

First, the hypothalamus, a small region in the brain, releases stress hormones such as adrenaline and cortisol into the bloodstream. These hormones increase heart rate, blood pressure, and respiration, providing a burst of energy to prepare for action.

Simultaneously, the sympathetic nervous system is activated, causing the pupils to dilate, enhancing vision, and increasing the sensitivity of our senses. This heightened awareness helps us detect potential threats more effectively.

The increased heart rate and blood pressure redirect blood flow to the muscles, enabling them to contract more efficiently. This allows for quick movements and increased strength, aiding in fighting or fleeing from the perceived threat.

Additionally, fear can lead to changes in our digestive system, as blood flow is redirected away from non-essential functions like digestion. This can cause a decrease in appetite or a feeling of butterflies in the stomach.

Fear also affects our cognition and decision-making. The prefrontal cortex, responsible for rational thinking and decision-making, may be temporarily impaired during fear responses. This can lead to impulsive or instinctive reactions rather than well-thought-out responses.

Once the threat is perceived to be over or the fear subsides, the parasympathetic nervous system kicks in, helping the body return to its normal state. It reduces heart rate, blood pressure, and stress hormone levels, allowing the body to relax.

It's important to note that fear responses can vary from person to person, and some individuals may have different physiological reactions or coping mechanisms. Additionally, fear can be influenced by past experiences, learned behaviours, and individual differences.

This physiological response is commonly known as the "fight-or-flight" response. It is an automatic reaction designed to prepare your body to either confront the threat or escape from it. The amygdala plays a crucial role in this process by quickly assessing the situation and determining if it is potentially dangerous.

222222

Once the amygdala detects fear, it sends signals to the hypothalamus, which activates the sympathetic nervous system. This triggers the release of stress hormones, primarily cortisol, and adrenaline, from the adrenal glands. These hormones prepare the body for action by increasing alertness, sharpening focus, and providing a burst of energy.

The increased heart rate and blood pressure help deliver oxygen and nutrients to the muscles, enabling them to respond quickly. Breathing becomes faster to supply more oxygen to the body, while blood flow is redirected from non-essential organs, such as the digestive system, to the muscles and limbs. This redirection of blood flow enhances physical strength and speed, aiding in fighting or fleeing.

Additionally, the release of stress hormones can temporarily suppress non-essential bodily functions, such as digestion and immune response, to prioritize immediate survival needs. This response is adaptive in situations where quick physical action is required.

It is important to note that while the fight-or-flight response is beneficial in acute and life-threatening situations, prolonged activation of this response due to chronic stress can have negative effects on physical and mental health.

Increased blood pressure

Dilated pupils

Tense or clenched muscles

Goosebumps

242424

Trembling or shaking

Feeling lightheaded or dizzy

Feeling weak or shaky

Feeling a lump in the throat or difficulty
swallowing

Increased sensitivity to sounds or light

Feeling hot or cold

Increased alertness or hyper-vigilance

Feeling the need to escape or run away

Urge to urinate or defecate

Changes in facial expression, such as
widened eyes or a tense jaw

Increased perspiration or sweaty palms

Tightness in the chest or difficulty breathing

Increased startle response or jumpiness

Feeling a sense of impending doom or terror.

1. Increased attention: When we experience fear, our brain becomes hyper-focused on the perceived threat. This heightened attention allows us to gather more information about the danger and react accordingly.

2. Memory consolidation: Fearful events are often stored in our memory more vividly and for longer periods. This is because the amygdala, a part of the brain involved in processing emotions, works closely with the hippocampus, which is responsible for forming and consolidating memories. The amygdala signals the hippocampus to pay special attention to fear-related information, leading to stronger memory formation.

3. Emotional response: Fear can also impact our emotional responses. When we encounter a fear-inducing event, the amygdala triggers the release of stress hormones like adrenaline and cortisol. These hormones prepare our body for a fight-or-flight response, increasing heart rate, blood pressure, and alertness. This physiological response can influence our thinking and decision-making processes.

4. Cognitive biases: Fear can also lead to cognitive biases, which are systematic errors in thinking that can affect our judgment and decision-making. For example, the fear of a specific event or outcome may cause us to overestimate its likelihood or severity, leading to irrational or exaggerated responses.

Overall, fear can have a significant impact on our thinking processes, influencing our attention, memory, emotional responses, and cognitive biases. Understanding how fear affects our brain can help us better manage and cope with fearful situations.

How fear affects our thinking

Fear can have a significant impact on our thinking and decision-making processes. Here are some ways in which fear can affect our thinking:

1. Tunnel vision: When we are afraid, our focus narrows down to the source of fear, causing us to overlook other important information or perspectives. This can limit our ability to think critically and consider alternative solutions.

2. Emotional reasoning: Fear can cloud our judgment and lead us to make decisions based on our emotions rather than rational thinking. We may become more prone to making impulsive or irrational choices when driven by fear.

3. Cognitive biases: Fear can activate cognitive biases, such as the negativity

303030

bias, which causes us to pay more attention to negative information and overestimate potential threats.

Chapter 2

How to Change Your Perspective

Life is not black and white, but a continuum of different shades depending on who sees it and what they see.   What is a theory and how is it created? Every person has his or her way of seeing and interpreting things. It is not anything else but what you see that defines your world and gives meaning to your life.   There is the known, there is the unknown, and in between is the door of understanding. " Aldous Huxley Whether your life is average or good depends on how you choose to look at it.   Your thoughts, ideas, beliefs, and experiences shape the way you think about life, which in turn directs the way you think about others and the decisions and choices you make.   Why You Should Change Your Thoughts

Although many people believe that their thoughts about events are the only truth, the truth is that your thoughts are relative; Your opinion is relative; Your opinion is relative. This is your job; It may or may not be true. The reality may be completely different than you think.   For example, if your thoughts about others are selfish and jealous of you most of the time, then you will not reach out to them, you will not ask for help, and you will stay in your cocoon, hanging in the middle. On the other hand, if you think people are generally supportive and helpful, you will do anything to find mentors, learn from them, and advance to a more professional and personal level. So sometimes, to understand life and what is happening around you, you need to change your thoughts and look at things from a different perspective.   "There is no truth, only explanation." Friedrich Nietzsche The Benefits of Gaining a New Perspective When you only look at things from your perspective for a long time, this one-sided perspective can make you think.   Getting out of the usual way of looking at life and yourself allows you to get rid of mental

problems, enjoy other things, understand
things, and see problems from many sides.
It looks like You may find good or bad
ones, but it will cost you if you replace them
frequently.

Five Ways to Change the Way You Think
To change the way you think, you need to
think carefully to gain a new perspective.
The good thing about your idea is that it is
not fixed. You can change your thoughts
and change your perception of the world
around you. The internal narrative that runs
through your mind and influences your
thoughts, feelings, and behaviours. Most
people don't listen to what's going on in
their heads. If your internal narrative is
spinning like a Ferris wheel of negative
thoughts and that little voice is important,
see how it works and see if it can work for
you.

1. Don't think this is "bad background noise" because it's not. Failure to do so will result in disaster. When you see unfounded criticism directed at you, confront it. Challenge him now. So let go of negative thoughts and prove them untrue. With time and practice, you will be able to turn your enemies into friends and start looking at things differently. "The understanding of truth and reality are not the same. What we understand and what we see are different. "Yong Kang Chan.

.

2. Change the story you tell yourself. Most of the time, you don't know that your life is unhappy because of the story you tell yourself. "You can't live your life." Purpose: "You're not smart enough," "You have many shortcomings," "What if others reject you," " "You're not talented", "You're not comfortable", "You'll make a fool of yourself", "What should I do if others reject you?" There are countless examples like this. Get a reality check. Look back at your life and remember your achievements, past successes, and victories. Remind yourself how to cope with depression, how to cope with depression, how to overcome difficulties, and how to get through difficult times. Know that if you've made it this far, you have the ability and power to achieve your goals along the way. You have everything you need to become a champion and achieve anything you want. Once you stop lying and start telling yourself positive and encouraging thoughts,

373737

your perspective will change dramatically.
You will find yourself a new and ambitious
person who can achieve big goals.

3. Don't complain that the world we live in isn't perfect. So life won't be easy. Things go wrong; People make mistakes, you make mistakes, plans fail and things don't work out. These will happen. But if you only focus on the dark side and keep complaining, you will see a negative picture of life because you are creating your reality. "When you complain you make yourself unhappy, you leave the situation, change the situation, or accept something else as anger" Eckhart Tolle.

Do not complain about what you cannot afford, it works without purpose, without pain, and without time. Instead, start enjoying the things that align with your interests and the good people around you. When you focus on the positive When you think about something, you change your thinking and start to see solutions instead of problems and obstacles. Change your attitude and your life will change. " Kent, Germany.

.

4. Be kind. If you are myopic, you will miss the good things in life. Make it a habit to accept other people's thoughts, feelings, and ideas to understand the big picture.

Being open-minded means looking at things from others' perspectives and accepting new ideas and information. This will go a long way in helping you get rid of biases, misconceptions, and prejudices. Being open-minded can increase positive thinking, change old ideas, eliminate limiting beliefs, and improve the ability to solve problems effectively. It also helps you make informed choices and gives you insight into how you manage your life, thus improving your quality of life.

5. GET OUT OF YOUR COMFORT ZONE
Leaving yourself in a cocoon means continuing to do what you have always done, having the same ideas and beliefs. However, we live in a developing and rapidly changing world. What worked yesterday will not work today, and your faith and perseverance will no longer be relevant.   A comfortable place is a place where you feel comfortable and safe. But within the boundaries of known species, there is mediocrity because there is no room for growth.   To stay current, you must constantly update yourself, try new techniques, and take risks. This will help you change your thinking, allow you to accept new things more often, and provide you with endless opportunities to achieve your best and reach your potential. Conclusion Your perspective is the lens through which you view the world. By changing your perspective, you can change your life and change your game.   Victim or winner, failure or success, problem or opportunity; It all depends on perspective.

424242

Your thoughts are omnipotent; they may stop you or encourage you to chase your dreams; They can tempt you to trust your luck or defy the odds and turn the tables in your favour.   "The true journey of discovery is not about finding new lands, but about seeing with new eyes." Chapter: Marcel Proust

Chapter 3

Get out of your head a way to overcome fear

Get out of your head a way to overcome fear

To overcome fear, you must put it out of your mind.

1. How to Overcome Fear Overcoming fear means overcoming your fear response and using it to your advantage. Start by finding your niche. Here are some practical tips to help you overcome your fears and anxieties and live life to the fullest. All. Understand your fear. Learn how to overcome your fears. Like any plan, I wanted to know how to overcome my fear. What's confusing you? Sit for a few minutes and listen to your thoughts, feelings, and

444444

body. Practice mindfulness every day and
see how it changes you. Once you find
your niche, you can face your fears.

454545

2. Realise that fear can make you valuable.
Our Heart Tells Us: When you are anxious,
your soul is trying to tell you something.
Then change it. If you feel uncomfortable or
slightly uncomfortable, this may be a fear
that needs to be addressed. To overcome
fear, you must face your anxiety rather than
run away from it. Treat fear as a message,
not as a threat to your life. When you fight
for your rights it won't ruin your life. This will
be your friend in overcoming your fear. This
is the ultimate guide to help you realize
your potential.

3. Stay calm in the face of fear. Sometimes you want to act, sometimes you want to think. Overcoming fear can lead to behaviours that do more harm than good, such as binge drinking, binge drinking, or binge drinking. Next time you're scared, don't do anything. Sit quietly with your fear for a few minutes. I'm thinking about this. What does this depend on? Are you afraid of disappointment? Does the story you tell yourself show that you cannot overcome this fear? A few minutes of meditation can make a big difference in overcoming your fear in a positive, joyful, and powerful way. A. Set simple goals. Overcoming fear is often hindered by the small goals or tasks we plan for ourselves. If you want to change your situation, ask yourself: What do you want from life and what is life like? Do you mean "maybe someday"? Or are you working towards this goal? Is this progress? Are you willing to make the effort? The first step in overcoming this is to decide if it is a goal you want. Are you your if you reach this goal? I'm climbing, if you

don't enter will you fall? Dig deeper into your thoughts. What is the best result? Financial improvement or more money in the bank? Maybe you want financial freedom and the ability to travel wherever you want. Think about what your life would be like if you didn't take advantage of this benefit and compare it to what your life would be like if you didn't take advantage of this benefit.

" "Compass yourself with success. ". Tony puts it another way" The only thing you have to flash back is the goods you're going to witness in life." If you changed the word" must" to" must" and accepted all the exceptions, you are. However, it's time to rethink your priorities, If you're still doubtful of how to overcome your fears and put your pretensions into action. Those who concentrate on prostrating their fears and achieving their dreams are girdled by like-inclined people. These people will not only be people you look up to, but they will also push you to achieve your pretensions. To overcome your fear, you must raise your morals and allow others to hold you responsible.

4. Embrace Growth When you're hysterical. you tend to stay in one place. What if you make a mistake? What if it doesn't be? You start to believe that you can't do this, that you don't have what it takes, and fear is holding you back. One of the swish ways to overcome fear and anxiety is to adopt a growth mindset. It's not about achieving your pretensions and completing every step of the way. No bone

 is perfect all the time, so don't try to be. It's about conforming to what you don't know and continuing to remain silent; It's the base of the development of the mind. You will

recognize yourself when you try to overcome your fear. get back on track. There will be multitudinous trials and agonies. When you understand that the path to success is through growth and change, you will be one step closer to achieving your pretensions.

5. PainChanging the value of pain.
 likes pain. ultimate of us go to great lengths to avoid this. But pain is a deep teacher. Illness can be a path of growth if you accept that your life and your sweats to achieve your pretensions will be painful. When you release the pain of the trouble, it loses its power and becomes just another tool for prostrating fear. Everyone faces difficulties in life. It doesn't count whether your failure is particular or professional. What matters is the assignments you learn from these exploits and how you apply them to your future. Don't let the fear of the query of the experience control your opinions, decide to learn from painful moments to control your life.

6. <u>Find your</u> purpose. You have completed the work of your mind, found the real reasons why you are holding yourself back and decided what you want in your life. But prostrating your fear requires you to exercise these habits every day and make them a reality. Imaging pretensions is a problem- working. It's used by some of the most successful athletes, actors, and entrepreneurs, including Michael Phelps, Arnold Schwarzenegger, Will Smith, and women's soccer star Carli Lloyd. Visual targets set your pretensions; The flux of energy depends on your focus. Can be used for beginners, contemplation, or contemplation training. The important thing is that you see yourself as successful and achieve your pretensions. You will trick your brain into believing anything is possible. This is an important step to overcome fear.

7

7. Accept that you will fail What is your biggest fear about achieving your pretensions? They will fall. But like pain, failure can also educate us. still, you won't be hysterical about it, If you accept failure as part of success from the true morning. Failure can educate you on important assignments that can impact your future ideas. Not everyone can do this. A successful business owner. World leaders. notorious chef. Artists, scientists, and brokers.

. We don't talk about failure but we celebrate success. This creates the vision that you really can't fail. But part of prostrating fear is accepting that everyone in the world has failed on the trip to greatness, including those you know and respect. The sooner you realize that your fear of failure is getting in the way of your determination to complete a task, the sooner you can accept failure and move on. How you deal with fear is what sets you apart from others. Overcome obstacles Unleash the power within you, you will learn how to overcome your fear and stopcock into your inner strength.

Chapter 4

Master ingredients to great achievement

Master ingredients to great achievement

Critical fixings for great things come about. Numerous of us come with diverse plans, objectives, dreams, and dreams Tragically, numerous individuals come up short of attaining their objectives, implementing their plans, or taking the primary step toward realizing their vision. Why is this happening? How can we make sure we accomplish our objectives? Numerous individuals have attempted to reply to this address

A few individuals succeed in providing
guidance one way or another, and a few
me up short. In this article, I am attempting
to allow you the blue formula I used to do
this. I think setting an objective and
accomplishing the goal is different.
Looking or these points ought to not alarm
you, but ought to tell you that it may be a
formula that can be rehashed and utilised.
On the off chance that you ask after this
information, you'll ensure that the inquiry
about you will be effective.rectified In
scientific science, the ixings are 1 and 2.
This is often like making a cake. You'll
select to test yourself or take it after the
enlightening. One option is more
dependable than the other. So, what are
the five points that will offer assistance to
accomplish our objectives?

.

Component 1: Decide our objective You
must know where our ing. On the off
chance that you do not know your
objective, you'll never get there. Hone
setting objectives and choosing between
things that are important to you. The
objective ought to be the ultimate objective,
not the middle-of-the road objective Once
you compile a list or list of objectives, you
wish to prioritize those objectives One
problem is that we cannot settle all the
important things and let go of the
insignificant things. Keep in mind, that he
can't do everything, you've got to select.
The team that brings you the foremost
esteem and gets you through the fastest
should be your beat ed. I will present the
"science of values" in a later article.

Component 2: Communicating Objectives
Once you've made your choice and distinguished your objectives it's time to form beyond any doubt you and everyone involved remember that goal. Regularly some things halt us from the way we want to go. There's nothing off-base with changing heading, but there's something off-base with overlooking where you're going. Everything you are doing should be measured by what you need to attain. Forgetting these estimations could be a formula for disappointment. I rehash my objectives every day, week after week and month, to a month to myself and to the individuals who play a part in accomplishing them. This is often the foremost imperative thing in terms of pulling and controlling the truck in the same way.

Component 3: Make a Target Presently you know where your target is and I'vegot reports it to you or the unch I ter you. Are

595959

you doing you know? It is time presently to
see at the HOW. This is often the
arrangement.

4: Moving Forward The fourth element is where numerous people and organizations fail. numerous people start with a good, clear idea, but warrant the tolerance and provocation to" get it done." They hope to bear fruit before the seed has time to turn into a tree. Seeds need good soil, terrain, and care to grow. You should continue to watch and water until the seeds turn into the fruits you want. According to them, no matter what you do, the way to success is to keep your pretensions small and repeat your plans. The plan needs to be estimated and acclimated consequently. Success is a strong word. numerous of us follow him; the utmost of us would like to overcome this problem. Success means different effects to different people. Success isn't about getting from point A to point B. In this world, everyone wants to be successful, everyone wants a good and productive life, but wanting to be successful doesn't enrich your life.

616161

There's a big difference between
successful people and unprofitable people.
Successful people aren't at the mercy of
success. They know that nothing precious
comes readily and that success isn't as
easy as unprofitable people suppose.
Successful people know that when you
want a commodity from life, you have to
immolate the commodity to get it. No one
 can achieve the ultimate thing in life
without an immolating commodity.

5. I can not win. The elders said," If you want to win the competition, you must fight hard." This is true. Only rare calls can produce winners. Success belongs to those who work hard and have no bus. To become a champion, you must learn to fight with tolerance, courage, and determination. Success does not happen overnight. The road to success is narrow, bumpy, bumpy, long and full of ups, campo, and obstacles. To achieve the asked pretensions, it's necessary to learn to overcome problems and obstacles. He could not indeed do that one bit. Every failure brings you near to success; Every fall makes you advanced. Every failure brings you near to success because every failure hides the assignments of success. However, failure can lead to success, If managed and followed rightly. The life of every successful person is full of problems and failures. They're good and strong by fighting and prostrating obstacles. Lack of provocation can lead to depression. That is

636363

why the adage says" Failure is the pillar of
success in life."

6. Immolation is important. People want numerous effects in life, but veritably many are willing to immolate for them. Those who want to lose weight don't want to eat big fish and meat, those who want to be strong don't want to go to the spa and train regularly, and scholars decide not to study. I want to learn the necessary knowledge and chops. The further immolation the better.

Success requires immolation and one must be ready to pay the price for success. During the immolation, people's feelings will change dramatically. We face numerous problems in this trial; We're facing numerous problems. But immolation directly leads to the development of determination, strength, focus, trouble, discipline, and numerous other aspects of achieving your goals. However, you must make extraordinary offerings to achieve that thing, If you want to achieve a high position of success in any area of life. American pen Napoleon Hill said" Greatness is frequently achieved not by egoism, but by great immolation." thus, to achieve pretensions and dreams, one must be willing to immolate numerous effects in life no matter what. Big or small. You'll encounter numerous questions and tests on your way to success. A successful person is ready to immolate his time, plutocracy, energy, physical strength, particular and particular interests, and indeed his life to achieve success.

7. Mind decides everything. Success is fifty percent mind. Whether your thing is to become a great leader, a sports champion, a successful entrepreneur, or a professional, intelligence plays a crucial part in long-term success. Your brain power isn't a commodity you're born with, it's a skill you learn and develop throughout your life. Just like physical strength, some people can become stronger through knowledge, chops, experience, and conduct. Cerebral strength refers to one's capability to manage well with challenges, difficulties, and pressures and to do one's stylish indeed in the situation.

Brain power requires you to balance your studies and feelings so that together you can make opinions that will lead you to action. awareness means being apprehensive of your studies and passions and being suitable to work with them when choosing conduct. In other words, internal energy is about breathing, not breathing. Cerebral strength relates to one's capability to break problems, issues, and problems in work and life. Having a positive mindset requires determination and perseverance to develop positive diurnal habits that will allow you to succeed every day despite lapses and failures. Willing to take pitfalls, accept new challenges, and break delicate problems and gests. People with internal illness focus on the good effects in life and spend time with others who have internal illness.

. Character matters American author and motivational speaker Zig Ziglar said: "It is your character, not your talent, that determines your height." Our behavior plays an important role in our daily lives and will affect our future. If you have a good attitude, you are hardworking, you believe that behavior, and you will live the life that many people want. On the other hand, if you decide to live with a negative attitude, always expecting the worst and never being satisfied with what you have in life, you will see your inner choices reflected externally. When you talk about character, it comes down to choice; It's up to you whether your character is good or bad. There is no more. The biggest obstacle to success in life is not believing that success is possible. Many people do not have a full understanding of what they believe and what they can and cannot do. They cannot see the greatness in themselves and do not believe that they can achieve what they want to do. This is

the main reason why they don't set goals
because they don't believe they can
achieve them. Their behavior affects them.

9. Build Intelligence. Intelligence is nothing but the second weapon that helps protect, support, grow, and make us successful. Intelligence makes a person independent, increases self-confidence, increases self-esteem, reduces stress, increases self-confidence, helps a person represent the group, and ultimately enables him to succeed in life. Intelligence is very powerful and if a person learns an important skill correctly, he can be good and successful in life. The problem is that people fail to realize the direct benefits of learning a skill. They only realize the value of their skills later when they encounter problems. Once they realize this they will start dealing damage and maybe try to learn a skill, sometimes even trying to learn a skill. But most people don't learn because of a few important things. This cycle continues for a long time. As we get older, these skills become increasingly difficult to acquire. They think the difference is a lack of intelligence, but then it is too late to close the gap. You have no choice but to regret

why you didn't learn these important skills in your childhood. They pay the price for this throughout their lives. One of the most important skills to develop is reading.

1010. Action required. Shane Rounce
"Action is the key to all success." — Pablo
Picasso This means that you need to take
some measures to achieve something.
Dreams and hopes will not bring you the
success you are looking for. Apart from
dreams and hopes, simple things are also
necessary to create success in life. You will
see that many people in the world have
dreams, plans, and hopes but cannot
achieve their goals. To achieve your
dreams, you need a foundation to work on.
If you plan and do it, there is no height you
cannot reach. Success in everything starts
with action. The decision doesn't have to be
major or life-changing. The movement may
be small. Then, after completing this habit,
try something else. Again, it doesn't have to
be monumental. Soon these small actions
add up. These little things will be the key to
your success.

11. Stimulating Passion "Passion is power. Feel the power of focusing on something that makes you happy." — Oprah Winfrey Passion is an emotion or desire, the desire to have something or to do something. Happiness or happiness. Passion can drive people to create great things in life. This is important for every result in the world. Passionate people strive to achieve their goals in life, make the most of every experience, and never fail. When you follow your passion, you do not need to put in more effort. For example, when you work with passion, difficult tasks become easier. People should do what they like. People do many things but they don't like them. Passion is an inexhaustible talent that gives you the power to do something different. Hard work leads to success and success leads to success. Satisfaction automatically creates the motivation needed to motivate employees. Without the passion to work for a while, it will be difficult to survive in the long run. Positive attitude, thought, intelligence, wisdom, discipline, behavior,

747474

etc. traits lead to success, and following your wi often results in the biggest change. That's whresulthould follow your passion because that's where your heart and soul are.

Chapter 5

Great ideas for dealing with fear and your inner critic.

What is the Inner Critic? Your inner critic tells you all the reasons you're not good enough. It stems from pain at an early age when we may see or experience bad behavior towards ourselves or those close to us. As we get older, we forget to embrace and integrate our own and others' thought patterns.

1 . The confident inner voice is constantly judging and blaming. Psychological problems such as depression may develop from this dynamic.

767676

2. Negative thoughts and emotions associated with the inner critic can be significant sources of stress and self-harm. Anxiety is another gentleness that can be associated with negative internal messages sent by your inner critic. Do Insiders Help? Internal criticism can be thought of as a survival technique used to identify potentially threatening environments. It can also help avoid failure or embarrassment. Internal critics can also motivate people to move forward and achieve their goals. It can also tell you how you can do it better. Inner Critic Examples The voice of the inner critic can be louder and truer than the voice of the parent who shares it. These messages can also be reinforced by society, reinforcing the message that we are different, different, or incompatible with others. Examples of internal thoughts are: You're ugly You're fat You don't deserve this You're stupid You're fat You don't deserve this You don't deserve it.

3. Nobody tells you what you think or if you're stupid You don't care no friends You don't deserve the job You are a liar Effects of the inner critic The inn er inner can damage your self-confidence and belief. yourself and your intuitive ability create a constant cycle of self-blame. It can also lead to self-doubt. The poison of negative self-esteem can lead to negative emotions and despair, leading to heartache. Constant self-critical thinking can create negative thoughts and lead to psychological problems such as depression or anxiety. Sochi Society may send negative messages that may come down to people's gender, skin color, or religion. These words can make people feel different, humiliated, or isolated. Internal Critical Voices Experts warn that this could lead to greater consequences, leading to more connections. In people who kill themselves, these feelings sometimes range from self-blame to self-harm to self-harm.

4 How to Overcome Your Inner Voice. The truth is that your inner voice will never disappear, but there are steps you can take to express your voice internally and bring compassion and kindness to yourself. With greater self-awareness and guidance, you can work to distance yourself from your inner voice and block its ability to create negative messages and judgments. Schur encourages: "If the inner critic can be powerful, the voice of the inner teacher can calm him down. The critic never goes away, but we can learn strategies to reduce his damage and rebuild neural networks in the process. Working together to improve our health and self-esteem, we can help our critics over the years." As we develop, the teacher within us also becomes stronger over time. We must imitate his voice and train ourselves to avoid the discomfort that occurs when we stop criticizing ourselves, accept positive comments, and use encouraging words for ourselves. Do kindness When that voice comes, take a step back to express your

797979

compassion as you would to others. is empathetic to behavior, emotions, and feelings, as well as self-determination and self-reflection.

5. Consider Acceptance and Commitment
Therapy (ACT) ACT suggests that we
acknowledge and acknowledge the
negative thoughts within us rather than
trying to change them. We. The critic must
say something and then try to let it go.
Know that your inner critic is the talker and
try to distract yourself from it.

 Change your thinking from self-attacking to
self-supporting First, identify the negative
thoughts and beliefs you encounter. Try to
write these thoughts in the second person,
as if someone else were talking to you. You
can try talking to a close friend who likes to
have a better idea.

Try Cognitive Behavioral Therapy (CBT)
CBT is a short-term therapy that teaches
strategies to help change negative thoughts
about negative situations and relationships.
It helps people better control their emotions
and create positive results by turning

818181

negative thoughts into positive ones. 5. Know when your inner critic is coming Be active and identify places, times, situations, and people that may trigger your inner critic's voice. This will help you prepare for its onset. You can then develop strategies to change these negative behaviors.

6. Accept that your inner critic never goes away. Recognizing that we all have internal conversations with ourselves helps us control our thoughts, behaviors, and actions. There's nothing weird or wrong about this. However, you can change the way you interact with and deal with your negative inner critic. Transform your relationship from enemy to friend.

7. Think about negative things about yourself, trace the roots of these negative thoughts, and understand them deeply. Who does it remind you of? Are there events or situations in the past that led to negative thoughts and self-talk? Stay away from criticism and do it; This could prevent him from getting promoted and help you avoid pursuing him.

. Use humour as an intellectual defence.
Think of your inner critic as a cartoon or
fictional character in a movie or TV show.
Choose an action that you think is stupid or
stupid and do the wrong thing. Think about
it and see who you choose as the centre of
your main sound. Inner critics with these
characteristics are often dismissed.